QUESTION & ANSWER

QUESTION

& ANSWER

ALISON PICK

POLESTAR
An Imprint of Raincoast Books

Polestar and Raincoast Books acknowledge the ongoing financial support
of the Government of Canada through The Canada Council for the Arts
and the Book Publishing Industry Development Program (BPIDP); and
the Government of British Columbia through the BC Arts Council.

Edited by Lynn Henry
Text design by Ingrid Paulson

NATIONAL LIBRARY OF CANADA CATALOGUING IN PUBLICATION DATA
Pick, Alison.
    Question and answer / Alison Pick.
    Poems.
    ISBN 1-55192-623-7
    I. Title.
PS8581.I2563Q47 2003   C811'.6   C2002-911422-5
PR9199.4.P52Q47 2003

LIBRARY OF CONGRESS CONTROL NUMBER: 2002115800

Polestar / Raincoast Books
9050 Shaughnessy Street
Vancouver, British Columbia
Canada V6P 6E5
www.raincoast.com

In the United States:
Publishers Group West
1700 Fourth Street
Berkeley, California
94710

At Raincoast Books we are committed to protecting the environment
and to the responsible use of natural resources. We are acting on this
commitment by working with suppliers and printers to phase out our
use of paper produced from ancient forests. This book is one step
towards that goal. It is printed on 100% ancient-forest-free paper (100%
post-consumer recycled), processed chlorine- and acid-free, and supplied
by New Leaf paper. It is printed with vegetable-based inks. For further
information, visit our website at www.raincoast.com. We are working
with Markets Initiative (www.oldgrowthfree.com) on this project.

Printed in Canada by Houghton Boston

10 9 8 7 6 5 4 3 2 1

For Thomas, Margot, and Emily Pick.

"If to record is to love the world,
let this be an entry."

— Roo Borson

CONTENTS

Q

    &   A

Q&A

"And all the question marks began singing of God's being."
        — Tomas Transtromer

Who made peat-moss,
old man's beard,
soft green sphagnum two feet deep
where a weakened body
can rest? Rilke says,
love the questions
as though they are poems in some
other language. But where do we go
when we die? All night
I dreamed of your father,
hot and thin in
his hospital bed. Once, in the summer,
I kissed his cheek
and now I can feel he's crossed over.
Where are those trees?
Where is that clearing, cushioned
in moss? Could be a parenthetical
world, a world on the back of our own,
where time is light turned inside out
and held, like a hand on the heart.

I wanted to tell you I saw him
there, wearing his straw hat,
leaning on a tree. He didn't speak,
no-one by his side.
Is this world real? the silence asked,
but he seemed to hear
and caught my eye, raised
his eyebrow, and smiled. He smiled. Thanking
Rilke of the many locked doors,
I'll listen to Rumi instead: ask a question
and the marvelous answer appears.

> "Is it raining where you are?
> Are you watching? Is the rain the story now?"
> — Helen Humphreys

How the rain falls. How it
fills the dusk with its sound,

buckets, pails, brown clay flower-
pots rising. How it lasts. How

the umbrella, motionless bird,
stands on one leg by the door. How

you get wet. How the rain runs down
the back of your collar, spills off

the slope of your nose. How it is gentle
and clean. How it is enough. How,

by the window, the rain is the story
that belongs to you more than any

other. How you sleep with its song
on the roof, blankets tucked under

your chin. How you snore. How the rain
makes a shelter of wetness, how it gives birth

to the river, then rests. How it hangs off
the raspberry bush, delicate lace of

the fern. Promising nothing and
keeping its promise, how the rain comes

to the edge of your sadness. How
it doesn't lie. How it doesn't judge. How

it is not afraid to cry.

"Anyone for tea before the night falls?"
            — Gwendolyn MacEwan

Night falls early
at the edge of the time-
zone, darkness settling
like silence on the house

at the edge of the hill,
its cool, thin shadow
on the house of this silence,
but for a kettle boiling tea.

Cool, thin shadow of death
sinks in, darkens to a stain
around the kettle boiling tea. Below
this house, where grandmother died,

stain of the dark lake sinks like
a shadow through a lung to
the depths of this death. This house. This
evening, snow. It touches the memory

of the shadow on her lung, of
poplars like women — thin hair, thin arms —
evening snow the memory
of moonlight on her bed. Thin

hair, thin arms, her old woman's
breath, the way the tongue
of moonlight on her bed made
a softness that licked her eyes

clean. The way her breath
was a settling darkness,
a softness that licked the
night to an early falling dream.

"How is one to speak with the dead?"
        — George Seferis

Gently at first, each vowel round,
only the softest of consonants sliding
from your tongue. Like anyone else
they will want to be praised — note

the new haircut, try not to dote
on the clammy blue skin,
thin black stitches like elegant
cursive through the lids. Stiffness:

a phase. With time, the elbows
will loosen their knots, open to secrets
of tunneling worms, raven's
curious beak. Keep your eyes off

the torn, muddied dress,
the blood between the thighs.
And: do not say *the dead*.
Say *she*. Surely a woman deserves

this smallest of respects. Surely
a girl. You may feel stunned, heavy
in the head, your heart a bloated
tampon in the bowl. You may

be frightened by the slur of crusted
semen on her cheek. And the way
her new breasts, pale freckled cheeks
remind you of somebody else. Do not say

your daughter. Remember, the dead
are hearing-impaired — she will need you
to choke through the clot in your throat,
speak up. Clearly. She's busy. Watch

her now as though she were a ghost,
a wisp of a silhouette putting on
lipstick, turning her back toward you
for help with the zipper. Turning

for the door. How happy
she looks, her night, her whole life
ahead. Before it's too late, speak
like you mean it — say to the dead: don't go.

"Will it go on?"
       — Sylvia Plath

All winter, the endless
winter which refers to only
itself. To drifts of
garbage harbouring
at the gutter — what is depression
if not the pelt of sleet
on the sleeping bag over the grate?
You feel as homeless
as snow giving over
to the liquid it fears itself to be:
you walk to the lake
in a rain which insists
it will fall forty days, forty nights.

The river's body,
its current of blood,
knows the certain impulse
toward movement.
But the lake, landlocked,
has nowhere to proceed —
its mind is its surface
scuffed with waves
colliding from every
direction. At the edge,
in an eddy of bottles and foam,
a muddy gull
struggling at the storm.
No green sprig in its beak.

"What is inside the antique eye that photographs you?"
— Patrick Lane

Here is the photo I was too shy to take:
your face in faltering light by a river
gone dry. Behind, the mountains,
season's first snow, a cliff-side
eroded until only its arm-bones

remained. We stopped for a smoke in view
of the columns, straight pillared reach
against backdrop of sky — and you,
your mouth, the rise of your chest, even
your breath seemed to heighten. I remember

the riverbed scattered with rocks —
a handful of beads, a sentence-string
snapped — *jaw-line, photograph, cigarette,*
kiss, each word a flake drifting down
through silence between us. I wanted

to cup your cheeks in my hands, angle you
into the line of my eye, capture
some piece of a landscape too wild
to be framed. Instead the camera lay
slung over my shoulder, useless

as a heart against my ribs. In the shot
I don't have, you've crushed out your smoke —
mouth open, you're saying you don't know
where the trail ends. All afternoon, the view
of your hair, your forest green jacket

receding. Look back now through all
that expands: time, desire, a sad thinning light
to the west. And me with this lens
still pressed to my face: how long
I've been waiting. Now smile.

"Is it a refusal of desire (at which point, do we not refuse
memory too?)"
      — Erin Mouré

i.

First, the dream. You are my teacher. I wake
with a longing to learn and open your book. This,

the gift that the man beside me gave — your name, his love
on the page where the writing begins.

ii.

This is thinking turned inside out, ropy twist
of what's called the *gut*; umbilical cord

that joins now to later, tunnels food for a future
that waits to be born. You: a name that slips

from my mouth fully formed.

iii.

Later, we meet. *Teacher?* I ask.
Your nod is the curl of spine around gut,

the place where my dream is growing, breach —
the place where your feet point down, stretch, then start

their quick walk away.

iv.

Several things. First. I want you.
Next. I want you because of this man,

the curl of his spine around me in bed,
the hole he opens

between wanting and touch, between coming
and leaving and everything passing

between.

v.

You know how I feel and I know your
knowing, feel it

as fur on the back of my neck, animal
muscle, bone laid bare, skin split open

to black spill of guts, black spill
of words: o, you are so hard to read.

vi

This is the truth: there isn't one truth. A woman's
the next, next is the man, desire shunting

like blood through a vein, spreading out
in concentric circles across the flat stretch

of the skin. Claiming its space. What doesn't
fit: the book isn't yours, simply recalls you

because it pumps
in the same blue room in my heart.

vii.

First, the book, the day I unfold you
to find that the man beside me has asked

you to sign it. You, or another I wanted
as badly — love, best wishes displacing

the last, claiming the warmth of my bed.
Or not. Maybe all wanting sets up house

between the same walls. Landlord.
Rent. Rooms to get lost in, where a name

is mistaken for the hole of its absence.
You were long gone before I noticed

your hand on the page.

"Why should you turn?"
    — Louise Glück

Joy: I know you
exist — nerves, purposeless
hair, five fingers opening
the coat of intention,
slipping it slowly to the floor.
Body laid bare
in late afternoon, bed sheet
pushed down, forgotten
like the mind's twisted promise.
The body a path
bathed in light.
This is not a joke. I have seen
your packed dirt, your clear
open road as though
it were simply a matter
of focus, the stubborn repetition
of feet. As though we might choose,
having chosen, might follow
this through. It ought to be easy —

trail snaked with tree-roots
that insist what is reaching
is already anchored,
secure. Brightness ahead
glows like a basket
of sorrow, tree-trunks,
blood-blistered heels —
it ushers the robins, the heart-beat
of hummingbirds forward.
It ought to be clear. Too simple
to speak about blindness, burn,
to assign the beginning
of unquenchable thirst
to the sun. You mean what you say.
Your first invitation has lasted
so long as to fall into shadow
behind me. You shine, shine, even
as I close my eyes and turn.

"What colour's the future?"
    — Carol Ann Duffy

The future is blue. Squint hard
and it blackens: a bruise, sour plum,
at daylight-savings retreating,
its mouth in its hand. Is near.
Is the refusal to harvest the root:
carrot, parsnip, all troops deployed.
You know who I mean. The one
on the hunt, on the prowl, with blood
on his hands. The fate of the future,
make no mistake, the favoured side
of the coin. Don't forget fear
(o the future is here!): the rubble
and gray of the twin match-
stick towers ashing down.
Is a gas — burns orange, burns
white — a year that combusts half-way,
on the fourth of July. The future's
a palate of colours too foreign
to worry the tongue: cobalt,
azure, the future is clear,
the glass you hold up to the past
to make it make sense. Make do.

Make an attempt: put your
change in the pot. The future
is green, the green of a well,
the o of its open, its poison, its entrance
to hell. Is road-kill, rodent,
near-extinct reptile — the future's
a lizard that loses its tail. And
grows back a new one. Or doesn't.

"What can you believe in?"
        — Tonja Gunvaldsen Klaasen

After midnight a dog's far-off bark, the skid
of wheels across damp pavement are sounds
recalling silence. Wine on the porch. The space
between our bodies is the space between our mouths,
the circle of light that a single bulb throws and
blackness stretching beyond it. All day the news
of war and starvation: you burn the low fever
of duct-tape and posters: Please George Bush, don't
answer terror with terror. What can you believe in?

Here, the night seems to reach out for
nothing, plants on the rail unfurling their green,
wet sheen of rain still slick with each bead and
fingers of vines, blind with their growing, feeling
the way toward heat. They don't need an answer. Or rather
their answer's the rumble of thunder, the wonder
of clouds that wander like mammals, heavy with moisture
carried like pails to the blistering tongues
of the thirsty. Your wine. I watch

you angle the glass to your lips, quiet yard close,
a warmth on our shoulders, gentle connection of
tree to its shadow, rustle of wind through the leaves
to my hand in your hair. Come closer. Let me whisper
my love of your fervor, my heartfelt respect for your verdure
that multiplies air. Yes, I believe in the action of peace,
split-second leap between synapse and speech,
sky lighting up, heat-lightning white, the open and close
of that moment of seeing, that clarity.

"Tell me, what is it you plan to do
with your one wild and precious life?"
— Mary Oliver

I come to the desk in my flannel pajamas, carrying a cup of black
coffee. Print the last page, make some corrections. It's cold,
and the thermostat cranky. Put on a sweater, then take it off.
Out in the field, nothing needs changing: the field goes about
the business of dying with perfect belief in the spring. Last night

it snowed but this morning it sticks, coats the gravel driveway,
the road, in a ribbon of white all the way to the lake. Michael
has written, saying he doesn't believe the divine intervention
thing. Neither do I. But somehow the field is focused in frost,
somehow the stars go out and come back. Somehow the moon
spins on its axis, opens and closes its mouth without making
a sound. Now my lover comes into

the room, wearing long-underwear, sleep in his hair. He puts
on the Schubert. We drink our coffee in front of the window,
fat flakes of snow falling into the water. This and each morning
we try not to speak. Soon I will put my sweater back on, move
to the desk. This space, this silence, someone who loves me:
over the field the clouds shift their shadows. When the last
change is made I will sit by the blank paper, listening.

(STILL)

LIFE

Apple

You are born.
Of a hard dark pip,
of semen,
it hardly matters.
Already hunger for the white bread
of knowledge, the word
for this fire that knifes
at your lungs: air.
It shimmers, shameless,
in the delivery-room's glare.
Your fervent father
comes bearing blood: pink
champagne, roses, red-delicious.
Look. That first fruit split,
your legs spread.
A girl, they say: their saying
makes it so. Beyond
your gasping mother the apple waits.

Beef Fondue

I trip through Granny's birthday dinner,
clumsy in the country of four different
spoons, crystal glasses sprouted
like roadblocks from linen.

Sixty years ago she fled eastern Europe,
changed religions like courses
of a meal after sherbet
to cleanse her palate.

And God forbid we discuss it.
When I ask about her parents
Granny won't reply,
her eyes on the pot
of spitting oil, slender necks
of the two-pronged forks.

Tomato

There is no denying its resemblance
to your heart,
its paper-thin skin —
it gives in so quickly
to the slightest pressure
from the blade.

Split, its insides fare
no better, four chambers clogged
with pulp and seed
as though in the need
to keep on, keep on,
the valves collapsed
in a flood
of what once was called
longing.

You could almost weep
for its fumbled attempts,
the way it has missed
its own mark. Relegated to the world
of stir-fry and sauce
at night it dreams
of another heaven,
lolling in the fruit-bowl with plums,
holding the light.

Fear 1944

She lost her parents,
her home, religion,
but fear survived.
She locked it in her body.

Like a gas chamber she sealed off
every opening, eyes and ears,
pressed her lips together
to keep it inside,
her stomach swelling
until she couldn't hold it
any longer — she opened, then,
her cervix like a mouth
and the scream that tore out
was my father.

Orange

There's got to be one
in the whole wooden
bowl, an orange
assured of its place
in the sky, that knows
its own curve & its hue:
the sun mirrored back.
Committed to rising
as high. Feel it.
A thin film of sweat
but it isn't afraid
of your hunger, thirst, your
tongue: that tremble's
desire. The wanting, wanting,
& finally the touch
so gentle its shivering pleasure
might also be pain.
A knife through its rind,
the readiness to be cut,
to bleed,
which you understand.

Its juice as refreshing
as anything the sun
might have dreamed. Taste it.
Sink in your teeth. Get
married as fast as you can.

Her Riches

In England she left her shoes in the hall,
expecting a servant to clean them.
In Switzerland she hired a nurse
for the baby and spent afternoons
at the movies. A guard's black bullet
was payment for the man
who smuggled her riches into Canada.
Diamond rings, an ocelot coat
but it's the shoes I think about,
tongues lolling under their laces.
They look as if they're about to speak
but don't say anything at all.

Pineapple

Unlikely guest with
tuft of spiked hair, rough
knobby skin, the ace it holds
to its chest, the element
of surprise. Love. That first cut
spilling with wet evening light
that is water and sugar
in bed, their pale limbs
entwined. Your husband's
soft sheen, summer getting
sleepy, undoing of leaves
that reminds you love
means less gathering and more
letting go. As if it has been waiting
for you to give up the pretense,
admit your own need and bend
to the thicket, empty-handed. To open
your eyes. As if it has always
been there for the taking, camouflaged
light at the centre of despair,
slowly removing
its clothing for anyone to see.

Prague 1939

My father taught me
not to be afraid,
to speak kindly
and look people in the eye

but I have no words
to soothe my uncle
who buried his small face
when the Nazis mounted the train

who carried his terror of borders
for the rest of his life
like a passport
that named him.

Cantaloupe, Honeydew

Before you were tall enough
to reach the gate
your mother expounded

conception: the pip, the dank
fertile ground, the Peter
Rabbit watering can.

Like melon? you asked,
equating its bulge
with the one beneath

her dress; and she answered
yes. Revised anatomy —
too late, too late —

the notion taken root
in your brain like a seed
in the particular soil

it was born to.
Cantaloupe. Honeydew.
The life-giving flesh

pierced by your plundering
spoon: you were never
fulfilled. Your belly flush

while mother's swelled,
finally producing
your brother, his tiny appendage

so much like a watering spout.
And this morning, crouched over
the toilet's bowl

you touch the dark earth
of your husband's seed:
the cleft incision where
the pointed spade slipped in.

Depression

I come by it honestly,
an heirloom passed
from my father
and grandmother before me.

In the bed by the window
she stares at the ceiling,
pills untouched on the dresser.
Cancer uncurls in her brain.

She says she feels nothing,
the heavy deadness
which also weighs me down.

Don't worry, love, depression comes
and then goes. Soon
it will be over.

She says this to me.
And to herself.

Watermelon

A boulder.
A rucksack of rocks.
A suitcase injected
with lead.

This heaviest
fruit that you carry
rolls on its vine
like the child's floppy head
bloating the space
in your womb.

Denser by day,
it is boldness manifest,
expanding its cells in defiance
of pain, the ache
in the veins down your legs,

multiplying sweetness
as though shame
did not exist in the world.

Freedom, you think;
but you lug it along
because of its centre,
the vibrant pink flesh.

Because of its slippery black seeds.

While My Grandmother is Dying

Three days in bed
watching the cold sun
cross the wall, the ceiling,
fall into darkness again.

I cannot feel, cannot move —
a giant gray fist
presses down at my chest,
pinning me flat on my back.

On the fourth day I twist
to my side and cry,
tears on the pillow
like hard spring rain.

Then, the relief
I cannot explain,
like an orange must have tasted
to someone freed from the camps

like her eyes fluttering open
in the operating room,
delivered back from death
one last time.

Banana

Call him honey, call him
love, anything sending out
the high clear light

      that is yellow.
            Sunshine. So close

to white, the purest
of snow, granular
sand he toddles over, bucket
in hand.
      Sugar. Come back
from the edge, my darling,
      my dear,

and he does, brandishing mud
like a flower,
stacking your name like a tenuous
tower of blocks:
ma ma ma MA.

Call this true love.

Even on the longest of cloistered
afternoons when he reigns
in his highchair (call him
The King), the tin cup
        dumped back onto the floor, banana
pushed back through his teeth
as though through a sieve;
        in your mouth
the names clatter —
        Sweet Pea, Sweet Cake —
like the rattle he shakes in his fist.
As though he desires
to be nothing
but the clear yellow light

he knows himself to be. Buttercup,
        Angel,
call him what he is:

your Baby. Your Baby. Your Baby.

Cortisone

The doctor increases the dose
and her speech comes back for a day,
the tongue a little sleepy
like a child just up from a nap,
words blurred together like a book
left out in the rain. She remembers
us visiting, her children and grandchildren,
asks whether Lester has plowed the driveway
and if her summer clothes have arrived back
from Florida. My father tells her gently to
talk while she can, to say the important things now.
She says the catheter is driving her mad,
it makes her feel like she always needs to pee
and could someone please bring her some
nail-polish remover? She wants to know who
phoned (Moira Bassett? Betty York?),
what it was they said, and when she'll be allowed
back on the tennis court. Silence, then, snow bleeding
thin veins of light through the window,

the rise and fall of a ventilator across the hall.
Granny shifts her body slightly to the left.
She folds her hands over her stomach.
She says: Friday night, when you were all with me,
I thought it would be okay to die.

Cherry

Cherries teach patience,
the necessary tongue-work
to separate sweetness from stone.

Dangling lanterns, they light up
abundance, the single branch
bent with their weight.

Not for them the cynicism,
the thick bitter rind
of grapefruit. Cherries stain
with impenitent joy,
more than a dulling of grief:

the child demands
that you wear each stemmed pair
as earrings.

But what of their murmurings
next to your neck
concerning the passage of time?

Cherries must keep the truth
to themselves. Like smug red Buddhas they hang.

For shannon bramer

No grief this fall until
I open your book
of suitcase poems —
they haul out everything
I thought I'd packed away

like my aunt,
jailed and beaten,
who fled across a border
leaving everything precious
behind.

Memory is empty
as her duffel bag
which hangs itself
from the cellar hook —
you remind me: slit the vinyl,
find the smuggled jewels.

Kiwi

What you have done
and what remains.
As though regret
might ripen
as simple nostalgia:
the brightest of greens,
bitterness giving over
to a clean aftertaste:
your husband curled
beside you, his nose
in a book, the child
grown so quickly
it must have been
a trick of the light.
The fruit on the sill.
You feel a fondness,
a certain recognition
of its muddy exterior,
the way it blends in.
It fits in your palm.
The bristling skin
so soft when you bring it
to your cheek.

Faith

An angel will lead you by the hand
into light. That's what the book said but
Granny wouldn't hear it — fair enough,
with what happened — she thought
she would meet her parents in Canada
then learned they never made it out.
Imagine the shock, the way you'd lose faith
if your mother was burned in a furnace.
Imagine growing old all alone.
In the days before death she tossed
in her sheets, glancing fitfully at
the corner of her bedroom where light
seeped beneath the heavy drapes. As if
trying to bring a face into focus.
Once, she asked softly, *Who's there?*

Pear

Queen of the fruit-bowl,
big-bottomed matriarch,
ripens in her own sweet
time. Holds out for ten
long summer nights,
fattening while the coffee
perks, then gives herself over
to what must arrive:
the opening outward
of light. End of contemplation,
end of isolation, this is the moment
the last stroke is painted,
the artist lays down her thin brush.
A still life, then:
tanned hands busy
splitting the pear
and you on the brink
of satiation.

What They Left Me

For Oskar Bauer 1880–20/1/1943
& Marianne Grünfeld Bauer 1894–20/1/1943

A passion for remembrance.

Two names on a monument at the synagogue in Prague.

The date they were deported to the death camp.

Their twenty-year-old daughter who got out.

Her son: my father.

My own small life.

The first light snow of winter, their ashes at my back.

Seed

Something holds you: a blanket
of dirt, a coffin of earth
in the garden, evening
descending. The chill

moves in like memory's fog,
cloaking the fruit, the flowers
in amnesia's haze. Daisies

lean over, chins in their palms,
trying to remember the secret
that waits to be told.

What were you before, they wonder,
then forget what they've asked, bending
to straighten the pleats of their pale-petalled

skirts. You turn in your sleep, dreaming
the fragrance of rain falling softly
on lilacs. They droop above you,
conferring in bunches, swaying
like a hypnotist's chain. *In your next life,*

they whisper, *in your next life
you'll be one of us.*

She Comes Back to Her Grandmother's House

The driveway winds for over a mile,
fields framed by poplar
and the lake far below
coming in and out of view
like a life that resists
an easy telling. Dusk chills to darkness
and darkness to fog, memory
of the day's heat gathers
in hollows, mists
into nothing as the car purrs through it,
elusive and useless
as speech, as a poet's
intentions. Cresting the hill
I know two things: grief,
and that the story was granny's
to tell, that my words put into
her mouth are mistaken —
how from a distance, poplar
is birch, fear is faith
or something else simpler.

Cancer, chamber, death;
the moon a single earring
in the sky. The empty house
lovely in emptiness. The lake
obscured by trees
though I know it is there.

THE RIVER

REFLECTED

And, what is more, I have spent
these bare months bargaining
with my soul as if I could make her
promise to love me when now it seems
that what I meant when I said "soul"
was that the river reflects
the railway bridge just as the sky
says it should — it speaks *that* language.
                                    — Jane Mead

Nocturne

1. Dusk

End of the summer, end of the day.
On the back porch a woman stands in silence.
In, then out, she drops each breath
like a tarnished penny into a jar.

Evening is pooling at her feet.
She might think of a woman, asleep
in the bath, the half moons
of her breasts on the surface. She does

not think of the man. She wipes her mind clean
of its failed arithmetic, claps the chalky brushes
in the wind. Language, too, blows clear
of the yard, snags on the fence, flies free:

there is inhale, yes, exhale, true, but the space
between holds no name. Lost
on the tongue like a word she might have spoken
when summer slipped out the side door,

or a letter penned in the future's
shaky scrawl, she can't make it out
for the shadows. Touched by gray
all things are equal: swing-set, hedge,

mountain ash drooping berries
over the garden's cold decay. The woman
shivers, rubs her bare shoulders, turns
for the sure thing of the house.

Pauses, and tilts her head slightly to the side.
As if trying to hear her own heart.

2. Dawn

A train whistle pierces the dark.
The woman lies still in her bed.
In, then out, she drops each breath
like a coin into the velvet purse of sleep.

Daylight is building in her chest. There's
a place she wants, a place she needs to reach
before night rolls over and yawns, dresses
and turns to its work for the day: polishing

sky with a cloth. A feeling that gathers at the edge
of her mind and then shifts, like a cloud
changing shape. In the space before waking
she thinks about sleep, its hands

closing thought like a book; her mother's
hands turning pages of a story,
turning off the light in the hall.
There is something she still can't

get hold of. A fugitive word, it flees
for the border, the barbed-wire fence
dividing the woods from the
wide open field of her mouth.

In catching it she hopes to be saved.
The way a woman will tease from a child's
garbled speech the threads she needs
to make meaning. The way she will lean

her ear down toward her body as if
trying to hear her own heart. But morning,
again, knows just its own song:
the slow breath, exhaled, the train's slow

whistle, longing buried under the tracks.
The dream disappearing like a mint
on her tongue: half-moon, quarter-moon,
gone.

Lullaby

If your daddy doesn't hear you cry out
listen for the sound of him wading in twilight,
casting and reeling in.
Slip into his tackle box with the soft tied flies,
curl into their cradle of feathers.

If your mother doesn't come when you call
go down to the fire
where she's cooking fish. Find the trail
of delicate bones, follow the spine into morning.

Even the great white pelican rests.
See: he tucks his beak under his pillow,
dreams of the trolling season ahead,
his nets twitching softly by his sides.

It's time to come home to the rushes
here at the river's edge. Fluff up your wings
like a good down blanket,
nest into this melody of sleep.

Infant Abandoned in High Park

Late afternoon, light through the branches is
a quiet the sleeping child breathes to. She waits

at the edge of some change: a cocoon,
a squirrel hoarding nuts in its cheeks,

the shiver of frost that promises self-
preservation. There's nothing

she wants. Her lips are a rosebud,
rooting at patience, the dark puckered nipple

of autumn, the thin milk
of love. She thinks her mother

is behind that tree, sneaking a moment
of calm. She thinks her mother

will return. Meanwhile the leaves
give over to wind — the rustle

and swirl of them falling, a mobile
of light the child smiles at

on waking. November, and she laughs
at the sun on her forehead, the shadow

of shifting that dapples across her young
skin. Now she is pulling the moment

to her mind, closing the clasps of memory
around it as her first: warm and content

in the cradle she's been left in,
her blanket clean, white as

a new fall of snow.

Driving: Shoulder Check

Summer evening, '79, our red Ford wagon
parked in the driveway.
Dad negotiates with the man
from the next block: *good on gas*,
room for the kids. I am four

and inconsolable. I sit on Mum's lap
and watch through the kitchen window,
crying hysterically.

The time we cross
out of innocence becomes
our meaning of *before* and *after* —
or maybe there are
many events, blind spots
to be checked.

Maybe the first loss
simply repeats like a tape
stuck in an old car's tape deck:

something outgrown
that I love nonetheless
being driven away in the night.

Driving: Who I Was

Driving north in winter twilight,
line of the highway like an open wound
in the snow's chest, the same line
I drove with you
in another, warmer, season.
While you tore over pavement at 160 clicks
we played that game
> *Would you still love me if I had six arms?*
> *If I burned down the library?*
> *If I was an ax murderer?*
pushing the limit of our love,
trying to find the place
it would break.

I remember the Rooney Bros. T-shirt
you wore, your raucous laughter when I asked
if you'd love me if I was a hedgehog
and I miss you, Matt, that careless confidence,
how recklessly you drove,
sure we'd never
get caught.

Night settles now, road scabbing black
like the details of us I can't get at anymore.
Hand on my leg, you sang Elvis Costello,
         Alison, I know this world is killing you
         Alison, my aim is true,
I remember that, the roar of summer
through the open window
and the promise of ocean
if we only drove
fast enough

but I forget who I was
sitting beside you,
laughing when the cop-car finally edged us over,
seat-belt loose at my side.

Wind Bound: Being Single

Wind so wild it woke me last night,
whitecaps roaring, I rolled over
in my sleeping bag lonely as this
Saskatchewan lake, half a country away
from every ocean

This morning the waves
crash against limestone, gray, white,
like snow blindness or
waking in winter
alone

My back turned, the tent sees its chance,
flaps its wings and bursts free of its pegs,
five silver question marks fleeing
the tundra,
what, when, where, why and *how*
solving themselves in their race past my reach,
leaving me alone with
the owl's soft call,
who, who,
the answer a name I can't hear
for the howl of the storm

Wind Bound: Devotion at Big Sky Lake

Ninety days out and everything I know
is here on this island
that fell from God's palm,
a penny into a well.
Jack pine, willow, crashing waves
have weathered my bones
as smooth as driftwood.
The storm keeps me chained to myself.
Canoe up on shore,
a slick of nylon's the only skin
between my heart and the wolves'
desire. The fifth night stranded
I bow my head and pray for calm water,
airplane smoke, a warmer jacket,
winter advancing and
no road out of here

The Rain's Hands

Restless tonight, I slip out the side door,
walk home as the rain starts to fall.
First, slow drops I can almost dodge,
then faster, like palms beating a drum,
the gutters swirling, rising at the curb
as at a river's banks

Months since I've touched another person
and the body only waits so long,
skin stretched taut, trembling in air,
liquid at the rim of a cup

All day the sky was swollen with heat,
now its water comes down …

Back home I strip off my soaked clothes,
lie perfectly still in the dark.
Thunder cracks and lightning floods in,
bathing each surface it meets:
the plaster walls, the floor,
the ceiling between me
and the rain's hands.

The Water's Skin

The moon sleeps in flannel pajamas.
The cry of a loon; the lake stretches out
under a duvet of fog. We paddle
our cedar canoe out of dreaming
up the thin river of touch.
Our boat is called longing:
how smoothly it skims the water's skin.

River

i.

The river's an eye looking inward.

A single lung, breathing.

Water, it wears through its blood,
its skin, hiding its bones on the shore
in a tangle of willow. There. Look again.
The smooth worn antler of grief like
a heart reaching out.

Next to your chest, the St. Christopher's medal
from your father before you began.
His hands over shoelaces, zippers, buttons,
catching your head on that first paddle down
toward light. Where is he now?

Alone is a circle of land at the river's own centre.
Turbulent arms at its sides.
Beach your canoe. Make camp
for the night. You know
what an island means, don't you?

ii.

The map is a child with a joke.
He hops on one foot, covers his mouth.
Why did the stream cross the road?

He gallops, somersaults, plays on the floor
with serving spoons, three metal pots.

His sister the river sings a blue line
while you gather kindling for light.
She noses toward you, flat on her face,
a bright green bow in her hair.

She wants to be lost. She wants to be found,
to rest in the shadow that muscles through current
like dreams muscling through sleep.

The map is a hand placed over the mouth.
The river will find her own way.

iii.

This for the girl with a boat on her back,
the blue-veined strength of her arms as
she brings it to shore. Her heart

is a dryness she's picked her way down,
forging a path through the boulders and now
she'll rest. Nude in the shallows
she washes her shirt, scrubbing and scrubbing
the cloth with a thin bar of soap.

She puts up her tent where the water hangs on,
clings to its banks in the summer's last light
like breath to the banks of her dreaming.

Love is a river worn down to a trickle,
a woman asleep on its shore.

iv.

The river flows backward, upstream.

Like memory it eddies
behind the mind
where trout drift silent as stone.

Tell me your losses, knee-
deep in water, casting
and casting again.

What you are hoping to catch.

Wildflowers

We walked through the prairie and you named them
for me, *columbine, aster, Saskatchewan lily,*
and the one that loses petals each night —
I forget what it's called.

All that week they opened between us
in the gravel at the edge of the road,
three kinds of raspberries, themes
on desire: *stemless, arctic, wild red.*

Does *chamomile* stand for the feel of the sky,
its hot sweet smell at night?
Or *buttercup*, dissolving on the tongue,
lighting up a face from underneath?

Or maybe *train*, the word roaring past us
leaving spikes loose in the ground.
You gave me one; I called it a peg
as in *tent peg* or *pegging you down.*

Which may be what I was trying to do
when you kissed me and backed down the drive,
repeating them silently under my breath,
lady slipper, clover, blue flax.

I committed them to memory, all except
the flower with a name that escapes me still,
petals falling on the cracked dry dirt
like a heart letting go of its love.

Birthday Repetitions

She says: make a wish before midnight.
One more hour. Careful, you can't take it back.

We're on the back roads, rise and fall
of gravel, moon a bowl of cream over fields.
Because we're near strangers, the night
waving silk, we play a game of *which do you prefer.*
Coffee or beer. Apples or oranges. Tell me
who you are. What you want.

Wanting: the hinge on which emptiness
opens, the voice pushing outward to name
each part. Fingernails. Lips. The soft click of tongue
saying *maybe*, or *no*, a door closing gently on words.
The hunger that comes with naming desire:
Apple. As if it were simple.

Two women drive in a car. You don't always get
what you want. To get what you want, you trick the voice
into speaking out for you.

Tonight the soul wants release from her skin, from words
that peel from the tongue unpracticed, like habit
or a recurring dream, to unfurl herself like the string
of a kite — she wants to reach up and let go.

Two women drive from the dark. One of the women
is me. I'm saying that wanting blocks the word,
sticks out its leg and trips it. The thing you don't choose

droops on the branch, falls to the earth
unnoticed. Cool, citrus spray of regret.
Dig your nails into what you rejected.
A ribbon of peel: shape it like something
you could still eat if you wanted.

Like breakfast or lunch. Today or tomorrow.
Teach me to love a bandage of darkness
without the sun bleeding through.

Two women drive toward light. One of them is
my soul. She worries the tape-deck, she leaves
through the window, she wants me to speak out for her.

A swatch of silk like a star receding,
a child's crayoned star in the morning. The body
high or the soul on a string, and who is
holding the end? The thing you pick is the thing

that rots, as if on your fingers a *wanting* disease,
a creeping darkness of flesh. The darkness of dreaming
the orchard at night, moon drizzling cream over fruit. As if
it's enough to lean on the gate, to look,
your hands in your pockets. A shadow slides sleek

through the tall grass beside the ribboning road.
Looks like a fox. Or midnight approaching.
Quick, what is it you wish for?

Washing Meditation

Late afternoon, monastery lights
gone out, I bathe in the darkness.
Snow out the window: a ghost of
what never was there. The scrape of a ladder
along the hall floor. For every monk praying
another one fixes the wiring, the fuse,
kneels at the sink reverently coaxing a torrent
of worship from pipes. The sound of

this service, of bathwater rising,
a slow soapy washing of skin to the tempo
of psalms. The dirt itself perfect,
the towel, the plumber, the sheen of things
broken, things mended. An old Chinese poet
bent over the desk of his breath. The run of his pen
across paper turns into the washcloth
across my bare arm, the arc of gonging
from the gold bell that signals a coming

of light. It slips through the window
and takes up the book, poems wide-eyed,
blinking so slowly, so still in the nursery
of tears. I read them out loud. My voice in
the bathroom the same as this silence
with shadow to give the words

back. Stand in the tub, dripping dry.
Snow like a memory of heat.
Weeks since I've seen a woman's body,
I open a circle of steam to myself
in the glass. Wonder who
I am seeing and what prayer could mean.

Prayer

An unopened letter on the desk.

Why is it never enough?

A list of your fears: afraid to be alone;
of dying; that words cannot save you,

that words are from Anna saying her mother
is dying. Long after her death.

Rattle of fear sucks dry your chest,
the smooth hard wings of a wishbone.
Wish for the fire, the curve of her hand,
her back stooped to blow on the ashes.
Wish to be back where the river's receded
like a daughter's fresh grief.

Grief's bone is broken and buried, deep,
in those clay banks of wanting, by the water
we throw it all into: coffee cups, longing, letters,
despair, but not like a dump, like an offering.
The clean shells of bodies, all we can give,
hair and a bit of torn skin. Mother, Mother,
we want back inside you — apprentice to waiting,
to being delivered, we want to lie curled in your blood.
Let blood stand for grief, its one sluggish vein
carving the banks of the body. Let grief stand for only
itself. You always want both: double scoop, double
rainbow: a second sad arc of thin light.

Anna asks if writing's like prayer,
the same focused love in the hands.

Sometimes there's nothing but the capital letters
of her name on the envelope.

Sometimes a boat, a paddle resting on it.

Sometimes, sometimes, there's grace.

Grace

Being, I have come to think,
is music; or perhaps
it's silence. I cannot say.
Love, I'm pretty sure,
Is light.
                    — Jan Zwicky

First you must learn that words come
from God. No bloody body has birthed them.

The first time you kissed me you held
a guitar. You said: *I don't want to be holding this guitar.*
I tripped on the table and fell against your chest.
Drunk, with light in my hair.

If I said *light* would you see this field, frost,
the cropped grass that holds it? Would you see the ocean
it turns to in eyes, scrape of stones on the shore?

My heart: a fine mesh sieving that water.
A valentine net catching nothing.
The fingers of air it slips through like hands,
groping the thick fog of wanting.

Once, a path I thought led to the heart,
the mossy log cabin of heart. The porch light was on —
flickering, barely — I climbed the steep steps
and jiggled the latch. I threw myself on the closed door.

There's one thing to say of the thing that you want:
as it gets closer, it burns.

Inside the cabin, God in her slippers, tea-leaves
spread on her plate. If I said *prayer* would you kneel
at her feet, let her comb the childhood from your hair?

Light, you said. *Light in each line.*

If I said *love* would you hold me?

There was fog over water that I took for night:
the lighthouse beam burned it away. I took that for morning
or falling in love. For the real light of the day.
Several things happened: the front door
was locked. I bashed my black boot through the glass.
A shiver of morning came from the trees.
You sighed your small sigh of light.

A sigh of words, turning out pockets,
poor and thirsty for light pouring down
like water, clear, like varnish or glue
on the wood of our hearts. On the guitar
left on the floor: your mouth on my mouth, the music.

God in her housecoat says to come in. She says
the back door is open. On the right hinge, *open*
means *closed* means *open* and both mean *love.*

A forest of love is a forest of longing, the soul's body
touching the human. First there was light, asleep in the field,
fingers of wind through its hair. That door swinging open
the first time you kissed me, a window for God to crawl through.
There's one thing to say about loving a human.
First, forget what you've learned.

Confluence

The open mouths of rivers where they join the sea.
The places where water comes together
with other water. Those places stand out
in my mind like holy places.
　　— Raymond Carver

For the first half of the trip we followed
one river, twenty-five days
of rolling barrens, the wild arctic tundra
unfolding around us,
the confluence ahead, floating,
a myth, like all that we'd ever,
ever wanted — once we got there
the rest would be easy.
Early each morning we'd ride
those waters, forward,
forward, the sun beating down,
horizon as clear as the rest of our lives,
ahead, forward, flies in our faces,
across the great lakes
where wind forced us back, forward,
for twenty-five days we paddled with it
ahead, like the dream of real love.

When we got to the confluence water
joined water. Both rivers glinted
like knives in our eyes and we couldn't see
the end of the first for the new start
of the next. You in the stern,
you looked at the map
then squinted around at the landscape, the angle
of sky. *Well, here we are*, you said.
On the count of three we stood up in the boat
and held our oars over our heads. Their blades
dripped gold in the faltering light.
Then we sat down. We didn't need
to turn ourselves, the current swung us
forward, around, this gone turning point,
thirty days left, we picked up
our paddles again.

Winter: Leaving the Farm

This is the fall. It is spent.
Let us watch it depart like the red
flatbed truck on the horizon, kicking up

dust. Not speed but sureness makes
the road rise, lends the illusion
of motion. Do you hear me? I'm saying it takes

almost nothing to make gravel fly. Kiss me.
Again. Because the valley between us
in bed is wider than we dreamed,

and growing. And new snow is building. Let us
stand in the wind with our throats tipped back, waiting
for the first flake. Meet me at the barn, its door

swinging wide on its hinge like an answer
unexpected. Like *yes*. We'll ride the John Deere
to the center of the field where the cow's breath will warm

your chilled hands. My poor heart will break. I will
sing you every love song I can think of while pulling
the last of the beets, blood-red, which we'll take

to the cellar where jars wait like feelings on the shelf.
Sealed off. A harvest of rhubarb, crabapples, pickles,
preserved. A feast for the winter. As if

the word *blessed* was to be saved.
Or *road.* The one with the pickup truck
leaving in dust: let that road carry us home.

ACKNOWLEDGEMENTS

Grants from the Canada Council for the Arts and the Ontario
Arts Council Works in Progress Program made the writing
of this book possible. Thanks to *Descant*, Oberon, *Arc* and
Exile, who recommended me for Writer's Reserve grants,
and to *The New Quarterly* for the same as well as for their
continued support.

An earlier version of the manuscript won the 2002 Alfred
Bailey Manuscript Prize from the Writers' Federation of
New Brunswick; nine poems from the title section won the
2002 Bronwen Wallace Award for Poetry and appeared in
The New Quarterly. Other pieces placed in, or were shortlisted
for, the *Arc* Poem of the Year Contest, the CBC Canadian
Literary Awards, the League of Canadian Poets' National
Poetry Contest, the Ralph Gustafson Poetry Contest, and the
Cambridge Writers Collective's contest. Some were published
in *Exile, Grain, Arc, Prairie Fire, The Antigonish Review,
The Fiddlehead, Room of One's Own, Writers Under Cover,*
and *Vintage 2000*. Thanks to the editors.

"Who I Was" is for Matt; "Confluence" is for Karl; "Prayer" is
for Anna; "What can you believe in?" is for Degan.

The Holocaust poems in "(Still) Life" are in memory of my
grandmother, Liska (Bauer) Pick, 1917-2000.

"Anyone for tea before the night falls?" is a variation on a pantoum.

I'm grateful to Tim Lilburn and the 2000 Sage Hill Fall Poetry Colloquium participants, and to the monks at St. Peter's Abbey, Fr. Demetrius and Br. Basil in particular. To the Saskatchewan Artists'/Writers' Colonies. To the Eastend Arts Council and the Wallace Stegner House where we stayed on two separate occasions during the writing. To Fred Schloessinger. To Stan Dragland and Suzanne Hancock for their feedback, Lynn Henry who edited the manuscript, and Anne Fleming who helped it find its home. To my aunt Sheila O'Connor and my late aunt Hazel Pick, and my family far and near.

I would especially like to thank Janice Kulyk Keefer, who knew what I was up to before I did, and who encouraged me to keep going.

Michael Crummey commented on these and earlier poems and taught me much of what I know about writing. Nicola Holmes supported me, as always, through the process. Degan Davis has been my traveling companion for the past three years; he sustains me in ways too numerous to mention. Love and thanks.

Sources for Quotations

The Roo Borson quotation on the dedication page is from *Water Memory* (McClelland & Stewart).

The Tomas Transtromer quotation on p. 11 is from *Selected Poems, 1954–1986* (Ecco Press).

The Helen Humphreys quotation on p. 13 is from *Anthem* (Brick Books).

The Gwendolyn MacEwan quotation on p. 15 is from *Gwendolyn MacEwan, Volume One: The Early Years* (Exile Editions).

The George Seferis quotation on p. 17 is from *Complete Poems of George Seferis* (Midpoint Trade Books).

The Sylvia Plath quotation on p. 19 is from *Ariel* (Faber & Faber).

The Patrick Lane quotation on p. 21 is from *Mortal Remains* (Exile Editions).

The Erin Mouré quotation on p. 23 is from *Furious* (House of Anansi).

The Louise Glück quotation on p. 27 is from *The First Four Books of Poems* (Ecco Press).

The Carol Ann Duffy quotation on p. 29 is from *Selected Poems of Carol Ann Duffy* (Penguin/Putnam).

The Tonja Gunvaldsen Klaasen quotation on p. 31 is from the poem "Bears," published in the literary journal *The Fiddlehead* (Summer 2000, no. 204).

The Mary Oliver quotation on p. 33 is from *New and Selected Poems* (Beacon Press).

The quotation from Jane Mead on p. 70 is from the poem "Concerning That Prayer I Cannot Make," published in *The Lord and General Din of the World* (Sarabande Books).

ABOUT THE AUTHOR

Alison Pick is the winner of the 2002 Bronwen Wallace Award, given annually to the most promising writer under thirty-five. Her fiction and poetry have appeared widely in magazines and her work has been shortlisted for contests, including the CBC Canadian Literary Awards. An earlier version of this manuscript won the Alfred Bailey Manuscript Prize (for best unpublished manuscript) from the Writers Federation of New Brunswick.

Alison grew up in Kitchener, Ontario. After earning her degree at the University of Guelph, she spent several years writing and travelling across the country. She now makes her home in St. John's, Newfoundland.

Question & Answer was typeset using Stempel Garamond. The Stempel foundry of Frankfurt-am-Main owned a sample sheet of Garamond's type, which was the basis for the Stempel Garamond that was released in 1924. This design has an angular, incised appearance which is unlike other Garamond types; it is also slightly heavier in weight, and is highly readable as a text face.